First Facts™

Animal Behavior

Animals Communicating

by Xavier Niz

Capstone press

Mankato, Minnesota

First Facts is published by Capstone Press,
151 Good Counsel Drive, P.O. Box 669, Mankato, Minnesota 56002.
www.capstonepress.com

Library of Congress Cataloging-in-Publication Data
Niz, Xavier.
    Animals communicating / by Xavier Niz.
    p. cm.—(First facts. Animal behavior)
    Includes bibliographical references and index.
    ISBN 0-7368-2626-2 (hardcover)
    ISBN 0-7368-5164-X (paperback)
    1. Animal communication—Juvenile literature. I. Title. II. Series.
QL776.N59 2005
591.59—dc22   2004000327

Summary: Discusses the various methods and reasons for animal communication.

Editorial Credits
Gillia Olson, editor; Jennifer Bergstrom, series designer; Linda Clavel, book designer; Kelly
    Garvin, photo researcher; Eric Kudalis, product planning editor

Photo Credits
Bruce Coleman Inc./David Madison, 9; Larry Lipsky, 13
Corbis/Karen Tweedy-Holmes, 12
Creatas, 19
Image Quest Marine/Peter Herring, 16
James P. Rowan, 11
McDonald Wildlife Photography/Joe McDonald, 8
Minden Pictures/Frans Lanting, cover; Mark Moffett, 14–15; Michael & Patricia Fogden, 17
Natural Visions/Heather Angel, 20
Nature Picture Library/Anup Shah, 5
Robert McCaw, 6–7

**First Facts thanks Bernd Heinrich, PhD, Department of Biology, University of Vermont in
Burlington, Vermont, for his assistance in reviewing this book.**

1 2 3 4 5 6 09 08 07 06 05 04

Table of Contents

Leaving a Mark 4

Communication 7

Using Sounds 8

Body Movement 10

Smells That Tell 12

Dance Communication 14

Appearance 16

Scent, Sound, and Dance 18

Amazing but True! 20
Hands On: Scent Trail 21
Glossary 22
Read More 23
Internet Sites 23
Index 24

Leaving a Mark

A tiger rubs its face against a tree. **Organs** in the tiger's face give off scents. The tiger marks its **territory** with these scents. Tigers also scratch trees to mark territory. They have scent organs in their paws.

Fun Fact!
Tigers also mark territory by spraying urine and leaving droppings.

Communication

All animals need to **communicate** information. Some animals use sounds to communicate. Some use smells. Other animals use body movements. Animals communicate to find **mates**, to find food, and to scare off **predators**.

Fun Fact!
Male indigo buntings sing to mark territory and to find a mate.

Using Sounds

Many animals use sounds to communicate. Male bullfrogs make loud, deep croaks. Female bullfrogs are drawn to these loud sounds.

King penguins live in large groups. To find its young, the parent penguin listens for its young's voice in the group.

Body Movement

Chimpanzees use their faces and bodies to communicate. They show fear with an openmouthed smile. A slightly open mouth means they are ready to play. Chimpanzees ask for food by holding out their hands.

Fun Fact!
Scientists have taught chimpanzees to communicate using sign language.

Smells That Tell

Some animals use smells to communicate. Ants make a scent trail between food and their nest. Other ants follow the trail to find the food.

Some fish also communicate with smell. If attacked and hurt, a minnow gives off a scent. The scent warns other minnows to swim away.

Dance Communication

Honeybees use dance to communicate. A honeybee's dance tells other honeybees where to find food. It is dark in the **hive**. The bees cannot see each other. Other bees lightly touch the dancing bee. The dance moves tell them where to go.

Fun Fact!
Searching for food, a honeybee may visit up to 1,000 flowers before returning to the hive.

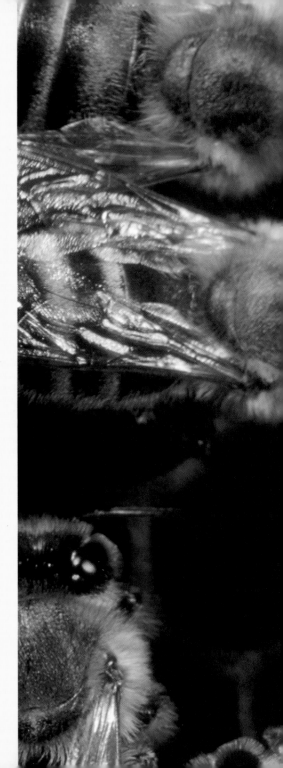

15

Appearance

Some animals communicate with **appearance**. Lantern fish have glowing spots on their bodies. To find a mate, they look for the same glow **pattern**.

Male ground anoles can fan out loose skin flaps on their throats. The fanned skin flap draws females. It also shows anger toward other males.

Scent, Sound, and Dance

Animals need to communicate with each other. Tigers use scent to mark their territory. Bullfrogs use sound to find a mate. Honeybees dance to tell where food is found. How do these dolphins communicate?

Fun Fact!
Dolphins are noisy animals. They can make clicking, whistling, squeaking, burping, and screaming sounds.

Amazing but True!

Knife fish can surround themselves with electric fields. They make patterns by turning the fields on and off. Knife fish recognize each other from these patterns. If a knife fish gets angry, it can make the field stronger. This way, other knife fish know to keep out of its way.

Hands On: Scent Trail

Ants lay down a scent trail between food and their nest so that other ants can find the food. Try this activity to see how ants communicate.

What You Need
ground cinnamon
garlic powder
24 small paper cups
scissors
tissue paper
24 rubber bands
pencil with sharp point
at least 2 people

What You Do

1. Pour a little cinnamon into 12 of the paper cups and a little garlic powder into the other 12 paper cups.
2. Cut squares of tissue paper to cover the cup tops.
3. Fasten the tissue square over the cup top with a rubber band.
4. Poke a small hole in the tissue paper with the pencil tip.
5. While other players aren't watching, one person creates trails on the floor with the cups. Cinnamon cups show one path and garlic powder cups show another path.
6. Have a second person try to follow the cinnamon or garlic powder path by smelling the paper cups.
7. Switch places and have the other person make the trails. Try making trails crisscross to make the path harder to follow.

Glossary

appearance (uh-PIHR-uhnss)—the way something looks

communicate (kuh-MYOO-nuh-kate)—to share thoughts, feelings, or information

hive (HIVE)—a shelter in which a group of bees builds its nest

mate (MATE)—the male or female partner of a pair of animals

organ (OR-guhn)—a part of an animal that does a specific job

pattern (PAT-urn)—a repeating group of colors, shapes, or signals

predator (PRED-uh-tur)—an animal that hunts other animals for food

territory (TER-uh-tor-ee)—an area of land an animal claims as its own

Read More

Jenkins, Steve. *Slap, Squeak, & Scatter: How Animals Communicate.* Boston: Houghton Mifflin, 2001.

Tatham, Betty. *How Animals Communicate.* Watts Library. New York: Franklin Watts, 2004.

Internet Sites

FactHound offers a safe, fun way to find Internet sites related to this book. All of the sites on FactHound have been researched by our staff.

Here's how:
1. Visit *www.facthound.com*
2. Type in this special code **0736826262** for age-appropriate sites. Or enter a search word related to this book for a more general search.
3. Click on the **Fetch It** button.

FactHound will fetch the best sites for you!

Index

anoles, 17
ants, 12
appearance, 16, 17

bullfrogs, 8, 18

chimpanzees, 10

dancing, 14
dolphins, 18

fish
   knife fish, 20
   lantern fish, 16
   minnows, 13
food, 7, 10, 12, 14, 18

hive, 14
honeybees, 14, 18

mates, 7, 16, 18
movement, 7, 10

organs, 4

patterns, 16, 20
penguins, 9
predators, 7

rubbing, 4

scents, 4, 13, 18
scent trail, 12
scratching, 4
smells, 7, 12, 13
sounds, 7, 8, 18

territory, 4, 7, 18
tigers, 4, 18

voice, 9

warning, 13